VOCAL / PIANO

ORIGINAL KEYS
for SINGERS

BEST OF
NINA SIMONE

D1597978

Photo by REPORTERS ASSOCIES/Gamma-Rapho via Getty Images

ISBN 978-1-4803-5276-6

HAL•LEONARD®
CORPORATION
7777 W. BLUEMOUND RD. P.O. BOX 13819 MILWAUKEE, WI 53213

Visit Hal Leonard Online at
www.halleonard.com

CONTENTS & DISCOGRAPHY

CHILDREN GO WHERE I SEND YOU

Words and Music adapted by
NINA SIMONE

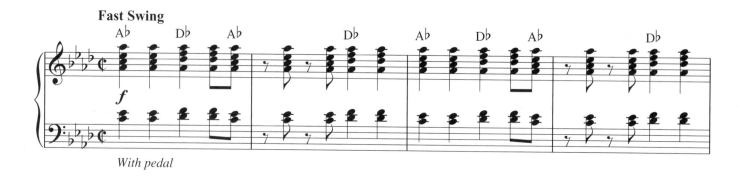

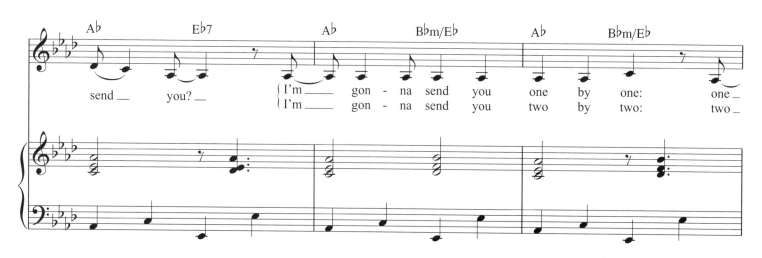

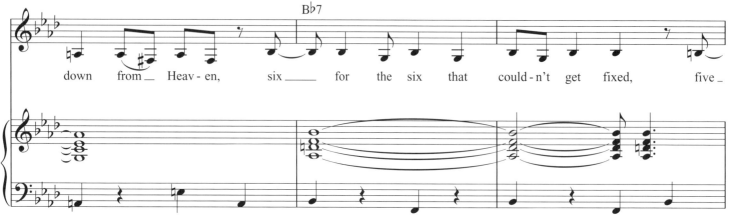

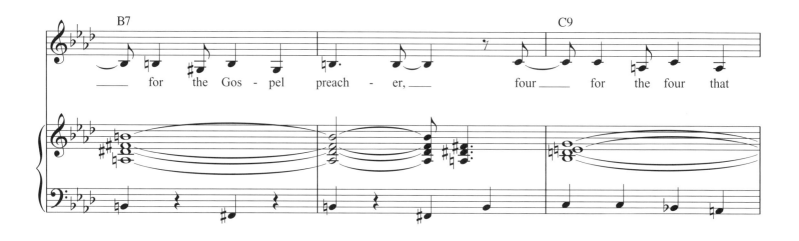

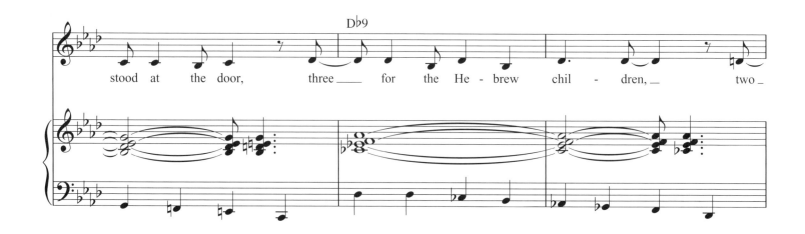

EV'RY TIME WE SAY GOODBYE

Words and Music by
COLE PORTER

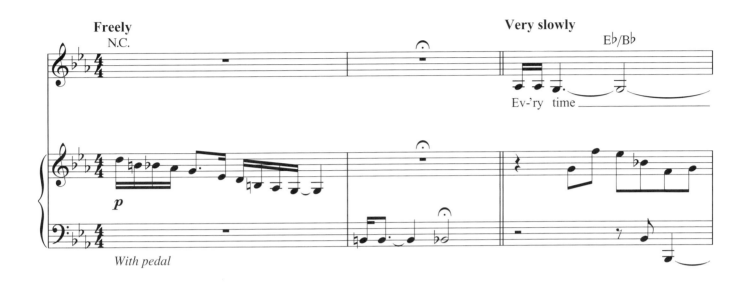

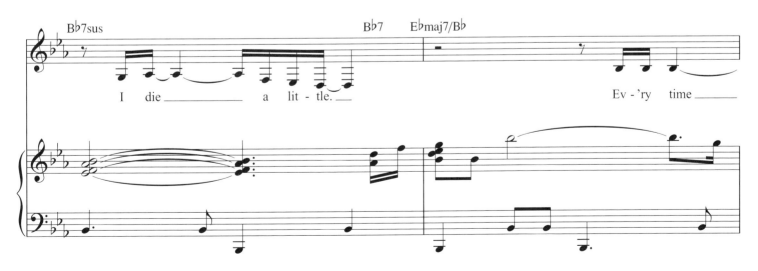

FEELING GOOD

from THE ROAR OF THE GREASEPAINT—THE SMELL OF THE CROWD

Words and Music by LESLIE BRICUSSE
and ANTHONY NEWLEY

Freely

Birds fly-in' high, you know how I feel. Sun in the sky,

you know how I feel. Breeze drift-in' on by, you know how I feel.

It's a new dawn, it's a new day, it's a new life for me, yeah. It's a

new dawn, it's a new day, it's a new life for me.

Ooh, ooh, woo woo woo, and I'm feel - in' good.

Heavy triplet feel

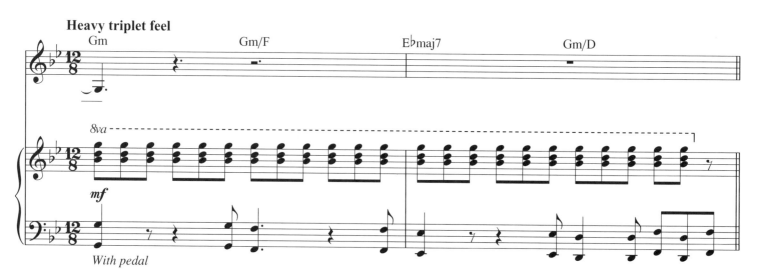

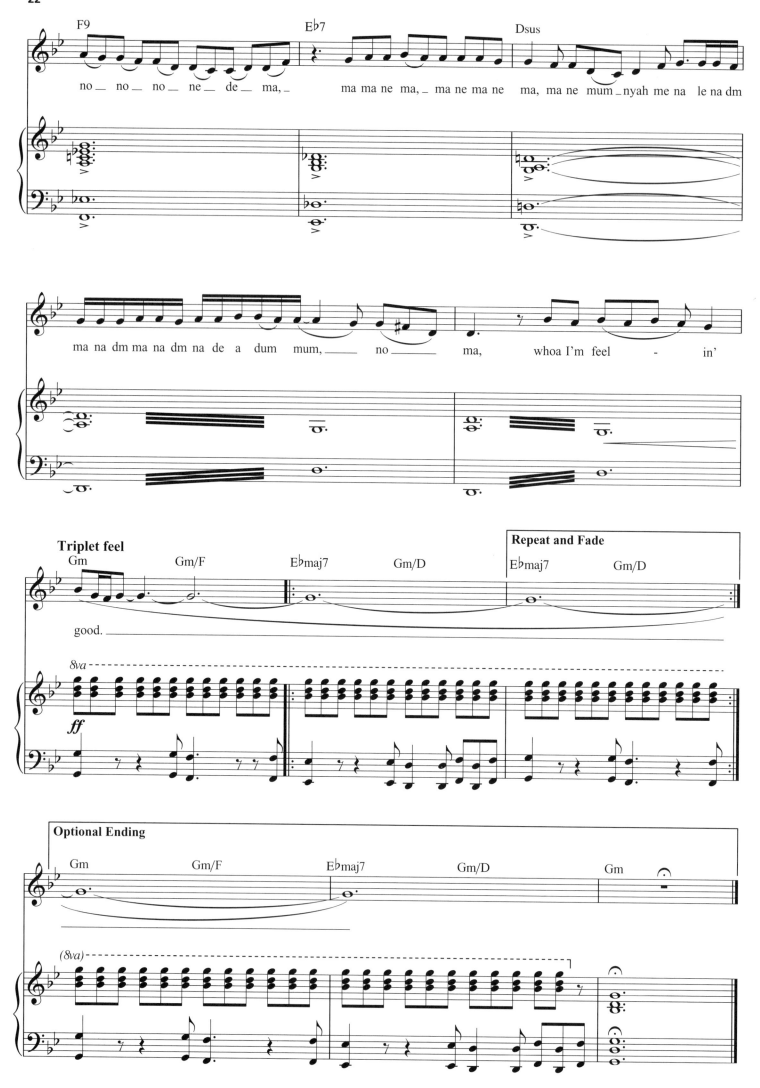

FOR ALL WE KNOW

Words by SAM M. LEWIS
Music by J. FRED COOTS

HE NEEDS ME

Words and Music by
ARTHUR HAMILTON

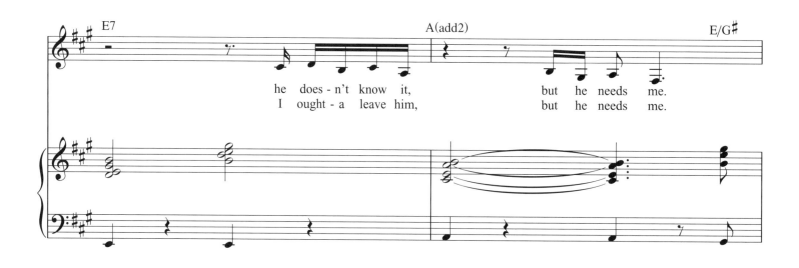

I LOVES YOU, PORGY
from PORGY AND BESS®

Music and Lyrics by GEORGE GERSHWIN,
DuBOSE and DOROTHY HEYWARD
and IRA GERSHWIN

I PUT A SPELL ON YOU

Words and Music by
JAY HAWKINS

IF I SHOULD LOSE YOU
from the Paramount Picture ROSE OF THE RANCHO

Words and Music by LEO ROBIN
and RALPH RAINGER

48

IF YOU KNEW

Words and Music by
NINA SIMONE

50

52

IT DON'T MEAN A THING
(If It Ain't Got That Swing)

Words and Music by DUKE ELLINGTON
and IRVING MILLS

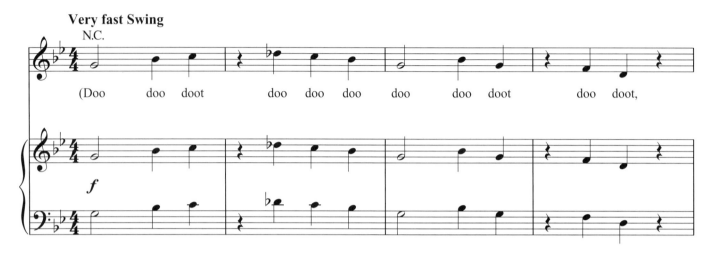

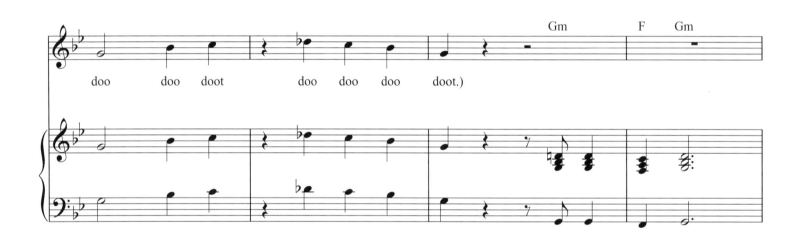

got - ta do _ is _ sing. _ (Doo wah, doo wah doo wah,

doo wah doo wah doo wah.) _ Makes _ no dif - ference

if it's sweet _ or hot, give that _ rhy -

thm ev - 'ry - thing you've got! _

58

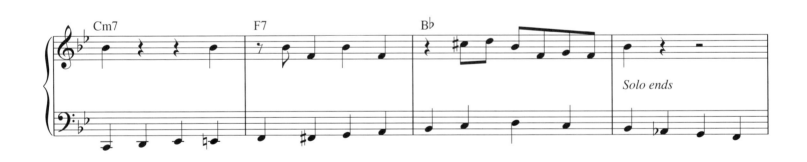

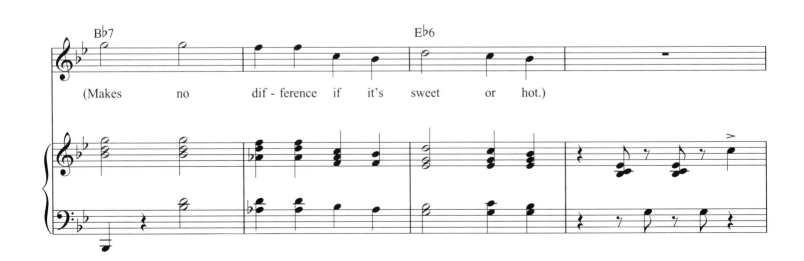

C7   F7   D7

(It
Solo ends

Instrumental solo

Gm

don't mean a thing, no, it don't mean a thing!)

Cm7   F7sus   B♭

Instrumental solo

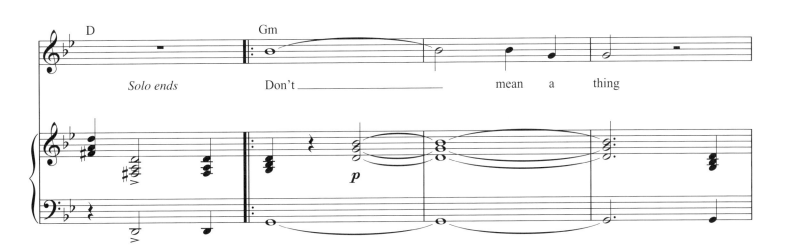

D   Gm

Solo ends   Don't _____ mean a thing

p

62

64

LILAC WINE

Words and Music by
JAMES SHELTON

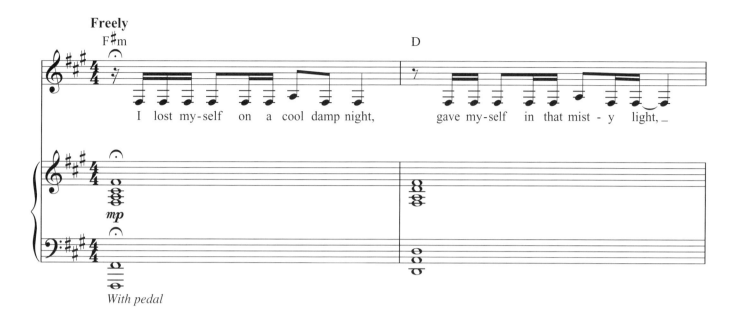

I lost my-self on a cool damp night, gave my-self in that mist-y light, _

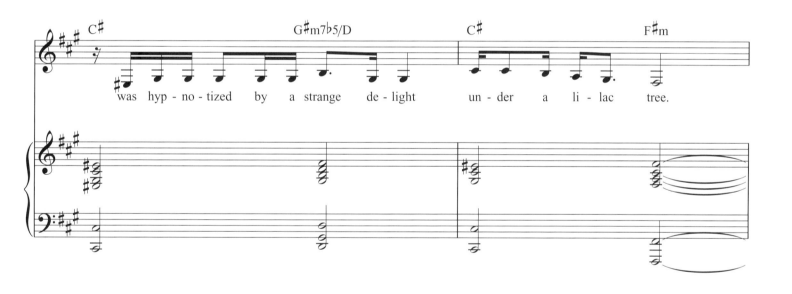

was hyp-no-tized by a strange de-light un-der a li-lac tree.

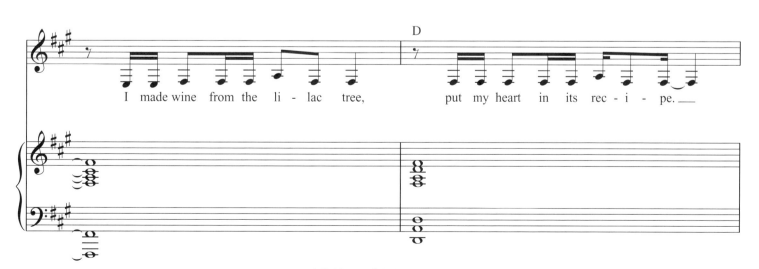

I made wine from the li-lac tree, put my heart in its rec-i-pe. _

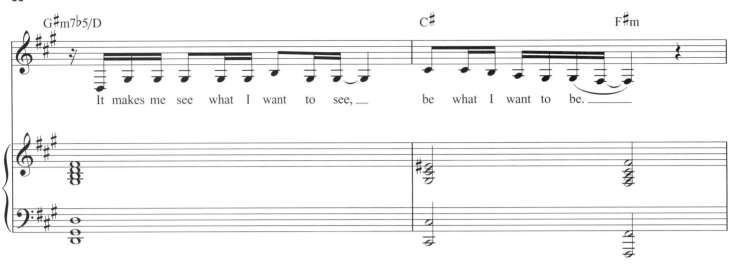

It makes me see what I want to see, __ be what I want to be. __

When I think more than I want to think, __ do things I nev-er should do, I

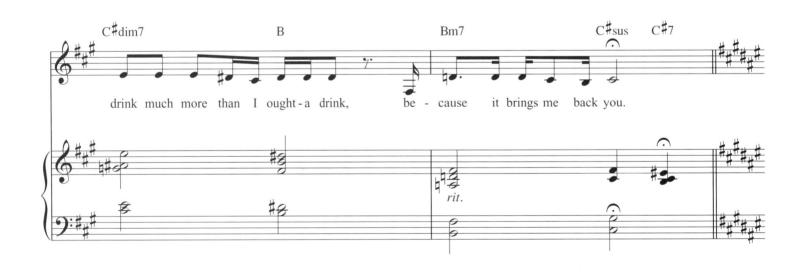

drink much more than I ought-a drink, be-cause it brings me back you.

Very slowly

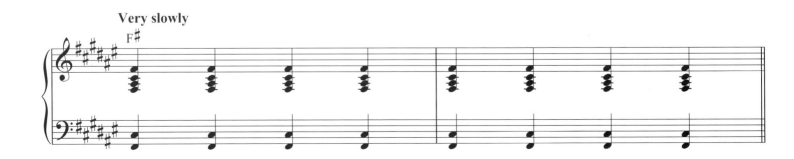

69

IT MIGHT AS WELL BE SPRING

from STATE FAIR

Lyrics by OSCAR HAMMERSTEIN II
Music by RICHARD RODGERS

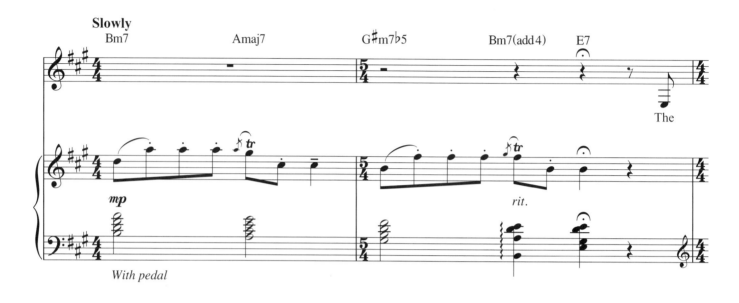

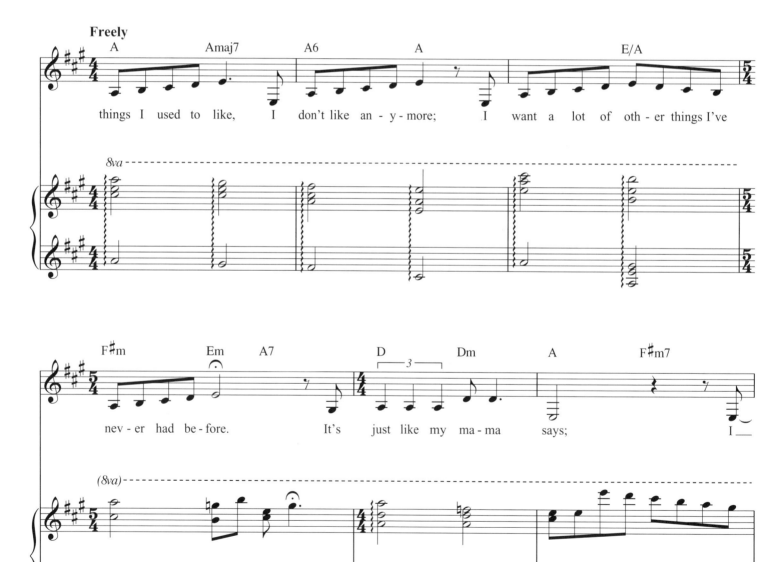

LITTLE GIRL BLUE
from JUMBO

Words by LORENZ HART
Music by RICHARD RODGERS

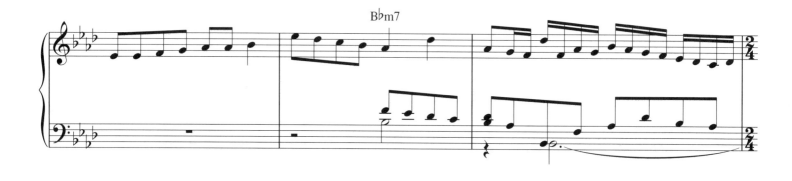

82

LOVE ME OR LEAVE ME

Lyrics by GUS KAHN
Music by WALTER DONALDSON

84

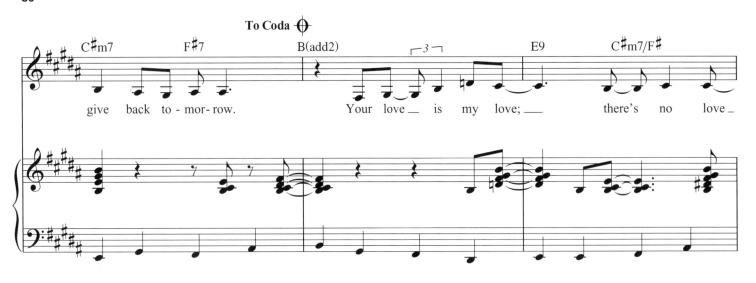

give back to-mor-row. Your love __ is my love; __ there's no love __

__ for no-bod-y else. *Piano solo*

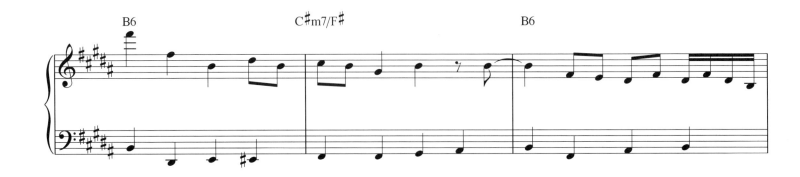

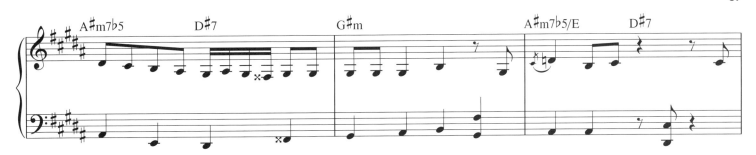

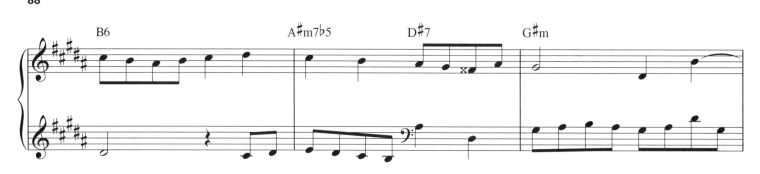

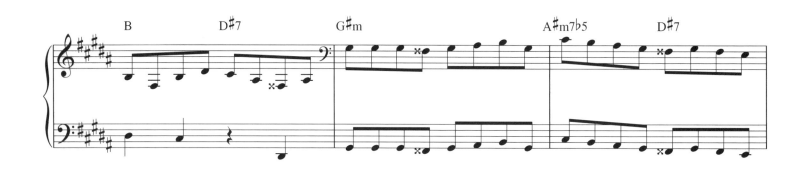

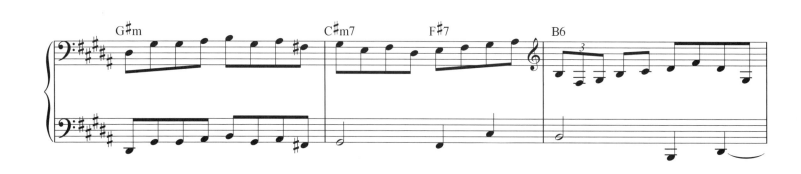

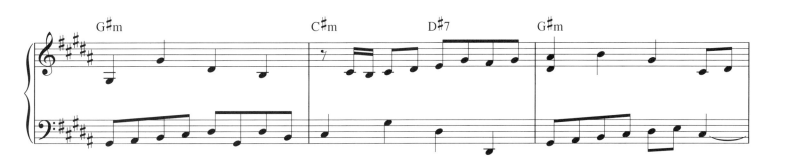

Swing eighths

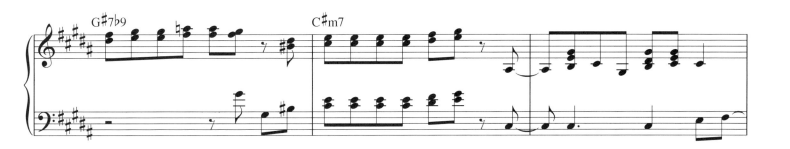

my love __ is your love, __ and there's __ no love __

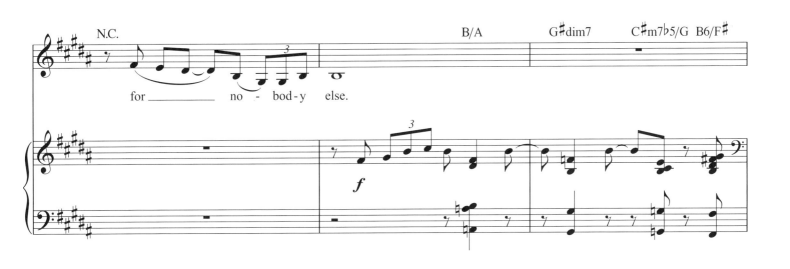

for __ no - bod - y else.

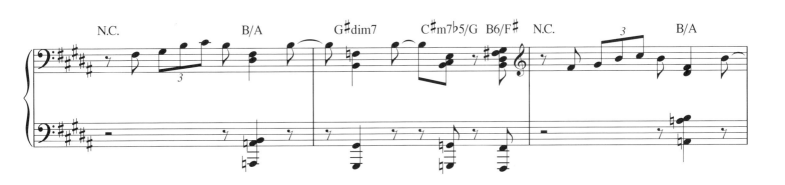

MY BABY JUST CARES FOR ME

Lyrics by GUS KAHN
Music by WALTER DONALDSON

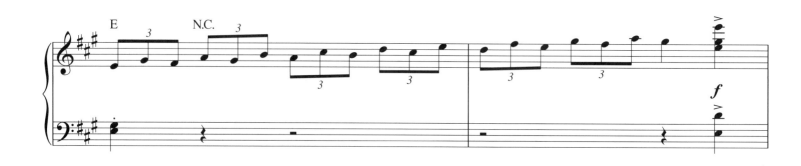

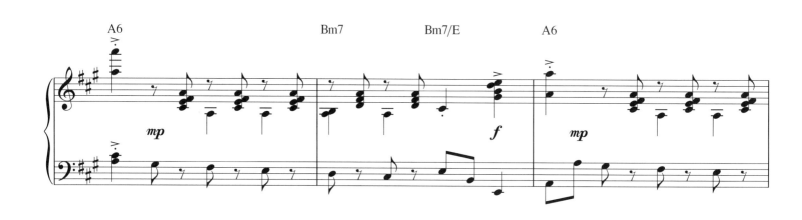

NIGHT SONG
from GOLDEN BOY

Lyric by LEE ADAMS
Music by CHARLES STROUSE

SOLITUDE

Words and Music by DUKE ELLINGTON,
EDDIE DE LANGE and IRVING MILLS

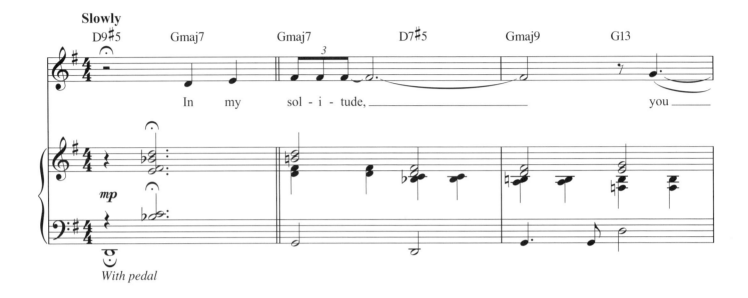

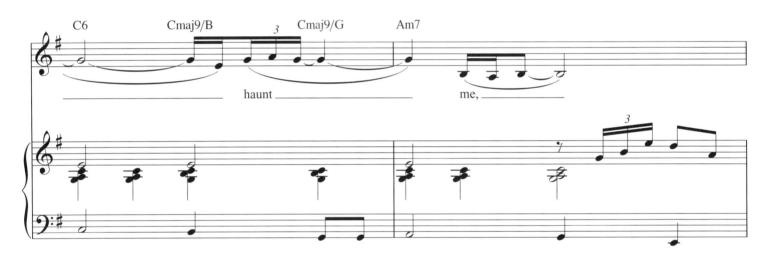

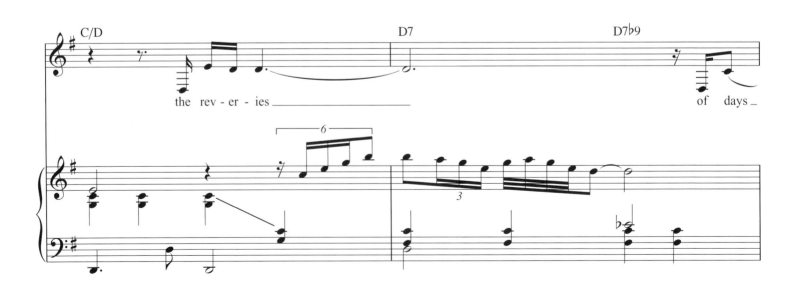

108

SOMETHING WONDERFUL

from THE KING AND I

Lyrics by OSCAR HAMMERSTEIN II
Music by RICHARD RODGERS

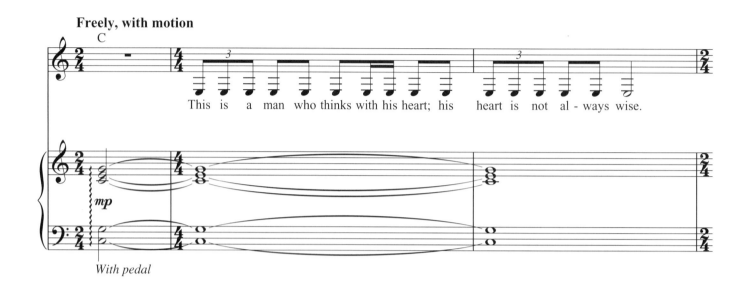

This is a man who thinks with his heart; his heart is not al-ways wise.

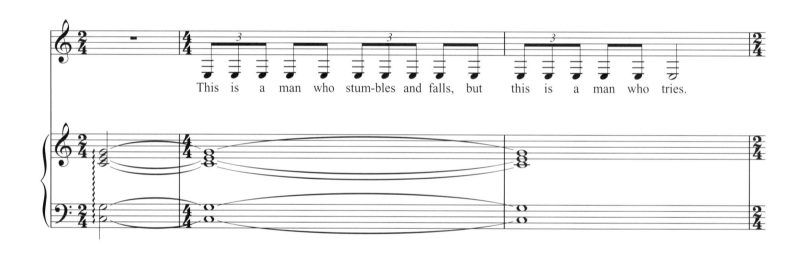

This is a man who stum-bles and falls, but this is a man who tries.

This is a man you'll for-give and for-give, and help to pro-tect as long as you

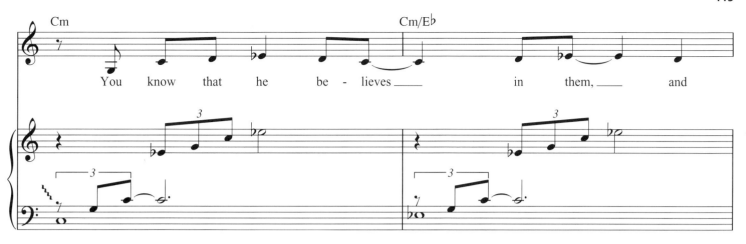

You know that he be - lieves _____ in them, _____ and

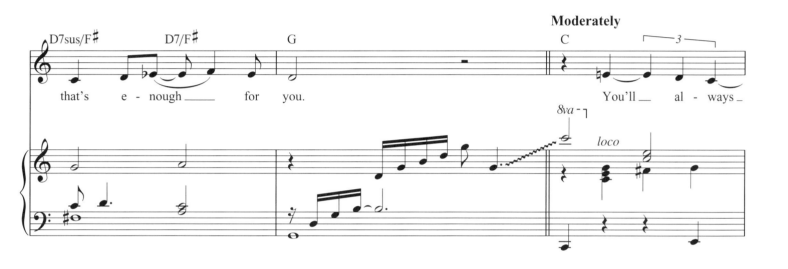

that's e - nough _____ for you. You'll ___ al - ways _

Moderately

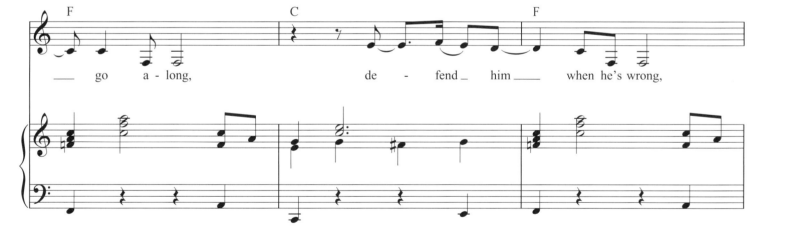

___ go a - long, de - fend ___ him _____ when he's wrong,

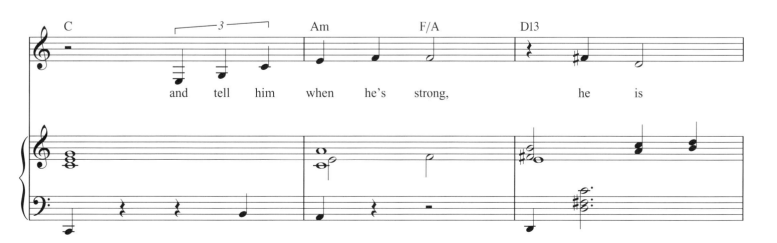

and tell him when he's strong, he is

TAKE ME TO THE WATER

Traditional
Arranged by NINA SIMONE

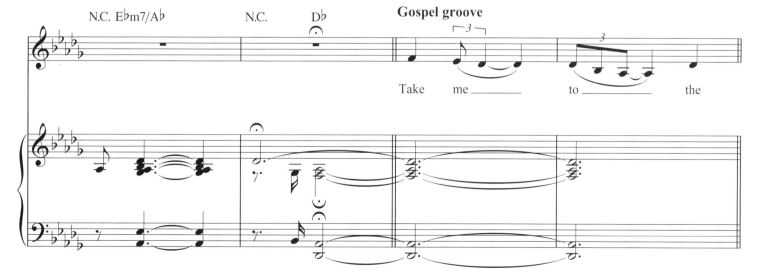

THE TWELFTH OF NEVER

Words by PAUL FRANCIS WEBSTER
Music by JERRY LIVINGSTON

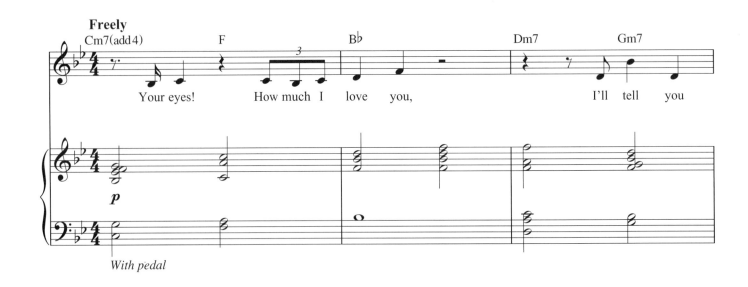

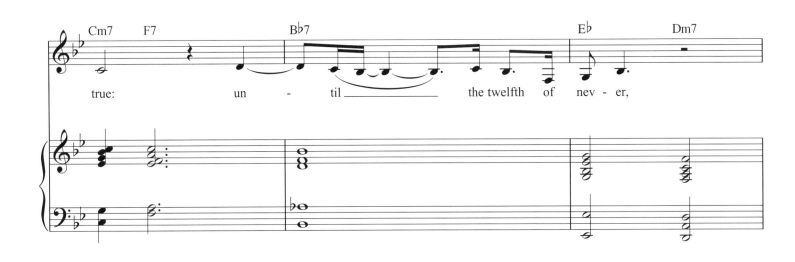

WORK SONG

Words by OSCAR BROWN JR.
Music by NAT ADDERLEY

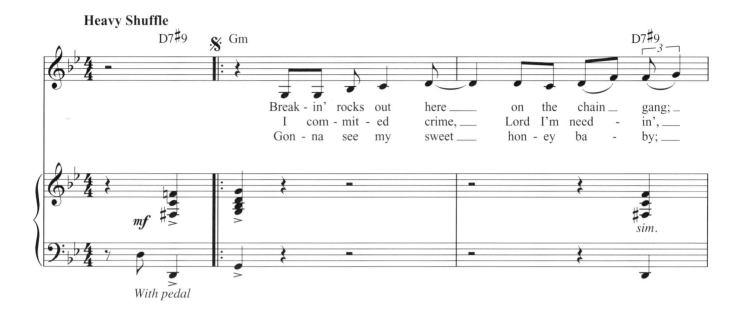

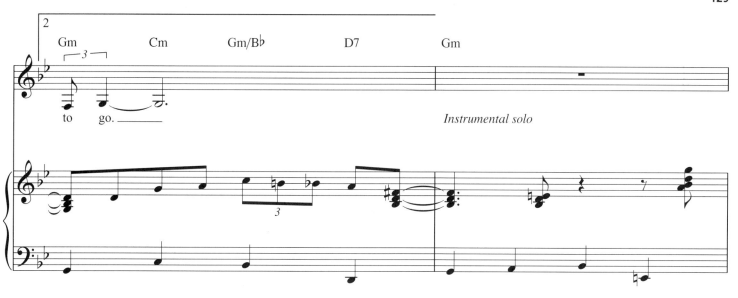

to go. _____ *Instrumental solo*

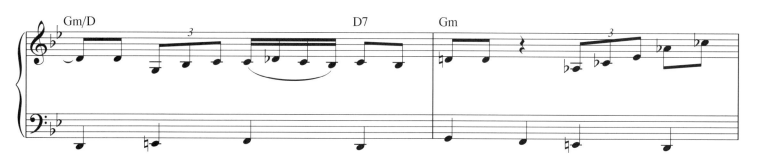

130

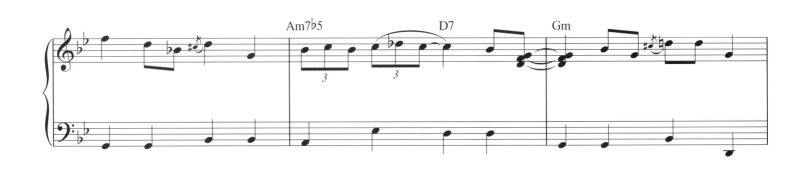

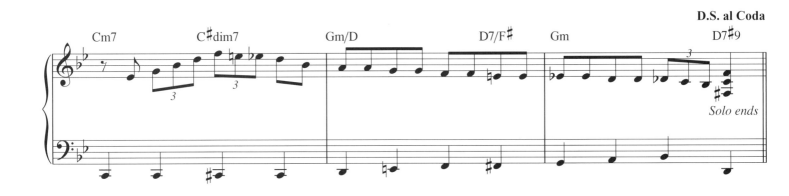

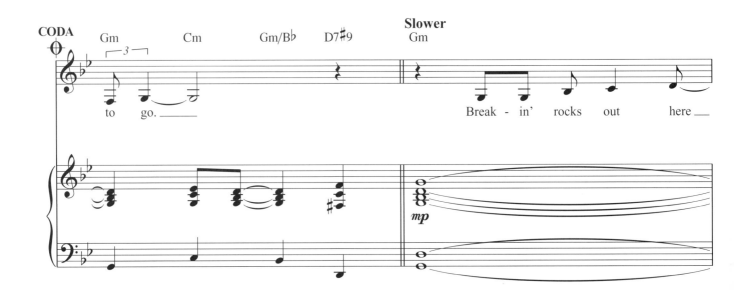

on the chain ___ gang; ___   oh,

Slowly and freely

I been work-in' and work-in', _____ but I still _____ got so

ter - r'bly far to go. _____

WILLOW WEEP FOR ME

Words and Music by
ANN RONELL

134

Bend __ your branch - es down __ a - long the ground and __ cov-er me.

When the __ shad-ows fall, bend, __ oh __ wil-low, __

bend, __ oh __ wil - low, and __ weep __ for __ me. __

YOUNG, GIFTED AND BLACK

Words and Music by NINA SIMONE
and WELDON IRVINE

Pro Vocal® Series
SONGBOOK & SOUND-ALIKE CD
SING GREAT SONGS WITH A PROFESSIONAL BAND

Whether you're a karaoke singer or an auditioning professional, the Pro Vocal® series is for you! Unlike most karaoke packs, each book in the Pro Vocal Series contains the lyrics, melody, and chord symbols for at least eight hit songs. The CD contains demos for listening, and separate backing tracks so you can sing along. The CD is playable on any CD player, but it is also enhanced so PC and Mac computer users can adjust the recording to any pitch without changing the tempo! Perfect for home rehearsal, parties, auditions, corporate events, and gigs without a backup band.

WOMEN'S EDITIONS

00740247	1. Broadway Songs	$14.95
00740249	2. Jazz Standards	$15.99
00740246	3. Contemporary Hits	$14.95
00740277	4. '80s Gold	$12.95
00740299	5. Christmas Standards	$15.95
00740281	6. Disco Fever	$12.95
00740279	7. R&B Super Hits	$12.95
00740309	8. Wedding Gems	$12.95
00740409	9. Broadway Standards	$14.95
00740348	10. Andrew Lloyd Webber	$14.95
00740344	11. Disney's Best	$15.99
00740378	12. Ella Fitzgerald	$14.95
00740350	14. Musicals of Boublil & Schönberg	$14.95
00740377	15. Kelly Clarkson	$14.95
00740342	16. Disney Favorites	$15.99
00740353	17. Jazz Ballads	$14.99
00740376	18. Jazz Vocal Standards	$17.99
00740375	20. Hannah Montana	$16.95
00740354	21. Jazz Favorites	$14.99
00740374	22. Patsy Cline	$14.95
00740369	23. Grease	$14.95
00740367	25. Mamma Mia	$15.99
00740365	26. Movie Songs	$14.95
00740360	28. High School Musical 1 & 2	$14.95
00740363	29. Torch Songs	$14.95
00740379	30. Hairspray	$15.99
00740380	31. Top Hits	$14.95
00740384	32. Hits of the '70s	$14.95
00740388	33. Billie Holiday	$14.95
00740389	34. The Sound of Music	$16.99
00740390	35. Contemporary Christian	$14.95
00740392	36. Wicked	$17.99
00740393	37. More Hannah Montana	$14.95
00740396	39. Christmas Hits	$15.95
00740410	40. Broadway Classics	$14.95
00740415	41. Broadway Favorites	$14.99
00740416	42. Great Standards You Can Sing	$14.99
00740417	43. Singable Standards	$14.99
00740418	44. Favorite Standards	$14.99
00740419	45. Sing Broadway	$14.99
00740420	46. More Standards	$14.99
00740421	47. Timeless Hits	$14.99
00740422	48. Easygoing R&B	$14.99
00740424	49. Taylor Swift	$16.99
00740425	50. From This Moment On	$14.99
00740426	51. Great Standards Collection	$19.99
00740430	52. Worship Favorites	$14.99
00740434	53. Lullabyes	$14.99
00740438	54. Lady Gaga	$14.99
00740444	55. Amy Winehouse	$15.99
00740445	56. Adele	$16.99
00740446	57. The Grammy Awards Best Female Pop Vocal Performance 1990-1999	$14.99
00740447	58. The Grammy Awards Best Female Pop Vocal Performance 2000-2009	$14.99
00109374	60. Katy Perry	$14.99
00116334	61. Taylor Swift Hits	$14.99
00123120	62. Top Downloads	$14.99

MEN'S EDITIONS

00740250	2. Jazz Standards	$14.95
00740278	4. '80s Gold	$12.95
00740298	5. Christmas Standards	$15.95
00740280	6. R&B Super Hits	$12.95
00740282	7. Disco Fever	$12.95
00740310	8. Wedding Gems	$12.95
00740411	9. Broadway Greats	$14.99
00740333	10. Elvis Presley – Volume 1	$14.95
00740349	11. Andrew Lloyd Webber	$14.99
00740345	12. Disney's Best	$14.95
00740347	13. Frank Sinatra Classics	$14.95
00740334	14. Lennon & McCartney	$14.99
00740453	15. Queen	$14.99
00740335	16. Elvis Presley – Volume 2	$14.99
00740343	17. Disney Favorites	$14.99
00740351	18. Musicals of Boublil & Schönberg	$14.95
00740337	19. Lennon & McCartney – Volume 2	$14.99
00740346	20. Frank Sinatra Standards	$14.95
00740338	21. Lennon & McCartney – Volume 3	$14.99
00740358	22. Great Standards	$14.99
00740336	23. Elvis Presley	$14.99
00740341	24. Duke Ellington	$14.99
00740339	25. Lennon & McCartney – Volume 4	$14.99
00740359	26. Pop Standards	$14.99
00740362	27. Michael Bublé	$15.99
00740454	28. Maroon 5	$14.99
00740364	29. Torch Songs	$14.95
00740366	30. Movie Songs	$14.95
00740368	31. Hip Hop Hits	$14.95
00740370	32. Grease	$14.95
00740371	33. Josh Groban	$14.95
00740373	34. Billy Joel	$14.99
00740381	35. Hits of the '50s	$14.95
00740382	36. Hits of the '60s	$14.95
00740383	37. Hits of the '70s	$14.95
00740385	38. Motown	$14.95
00740386	39. Hank Williams	$14.95
00740387	40. Neil Diamond	$14.95
00740391	41. Contemporary Christian	$14.95
00740397	42. Christmas Hits	$15.95
00740399	43. Ray	$14.95
00740400	44. The Rat Pack Hits	$14.99
00740401	45. Songs in the Style of Nat "King" Cole	$14.99
00740402	46. At the Lounge	$14.95
00740403	47. The Big Band Singer	$14.95
00740404	48. Jazz Cabaret Songs	$14.99
00740405	49. Cabaret Songs	$14.99
00740406	50. Big Band Standards	$14.99
00740412	51. Broadway's Best	$14.99
00740427	52. Great Standards Collection	$19.99
00740431	53. Worship Favorites	$14.99
00740435	54. Barry Manilow	$14.99
00740436	55. Lionel Richie	$14.99
00740439	56. Michael Bublé – Crazy Love	$15.99
00740441	57. Johnny Cash	$14.99
00740442	58. Bruno Mars	$14.99
00740448	59. The Grammy Awards Best Male Pop Vocal Performance 1990-1999	$14.99
00740449	60. The Grammy Awards Best Male Pop Vocal Performance 2000-2009	$14.99
00740452	61. Michael Bublé – Call Me Irresponsible	$14.99

00101777	62. Michael Bublé – Christmas	$19.99
00102658	63. Michael Jackson	$14.99
00109288	64. Justin Bieber	$14.99

WARM-UPS

00740395	Vocal Warm-Ups	$14.99

MIXED EDITIONS

These editions feature songs for both male and female voices.

00740311	1. Wedding Duets	$12.95
00740398	2. Enchanted	$14.95
00740407	3. Rent	$14.95
00740408	4. Broadway Favorites	$14.99
00740413	5. South Pacific	$15.99
00740414	6. High School Musical 3	$14.99
00740429	7. Christmas Carols	$14.99
00740437	8. Glee	$16.99
00740440	9. More Songs from Glee	$21.99
00740443	10. Even More Songs from Glee	$15.99
00116960	11. Les Misérables	$19.99

KIDS EDITIONS

00740451	1. Songs Children Can Sing!	$14.99

Visit Hal Leonard online at
www.halleonard.com

7777 W. BLUEMOUND RD. P.O. BOX 13819 MILWAUKEE, WI 53213

Prices, contents, & availability subject to change without notice.

1113

ORIGINAL KEYS FOR SINGERS

ACROSS THE UNIVERSE
Because • Blackbird • Hey Jude • Let It Be • Revolution • Something • and more.
00307010 Vocal Transcriptions with Piano $19.95

LOUIS ARMSTRONG
Dream a Little Dream of Me • Hello, Dolly! • Mack the Knife • Makin' Whoopee! • Mame • St. Louis Blues • What a Wonderful World • Zip-A-Dee-Doo-Dah • and more.
00307029 Vocal Transcriptions with Piano $19.99

THE BEATLES
And I Love Her • Blackbird • The Fool on the Hill • Here, There and Everywhere • I Will • Let It Be • Michelle • Something • With a Little Help from My Friends • and more.
00307400 Vocal Transcriptions with Piano $19.99

BROADWAY HITS (FEMALE SINGERS)
23 Broadway favorites from their most memorable renditions, including: And I Am Telling You I'm Not Going (Jennifer Hudson) • Cabaret (Liza Minelli) • Defying Gravity (Idina Menzel) • Edelweiss (Julie Andrews) • and more.
00119085 Vocal Transcriptions with Piano $19.99

BROADWAY HITS (MALE SINGERS)
23 timeless Broadway hits true to the men who made them famous: Bring Him Home (David Campbell) • If Ever I Would Leave You (Robert Goulet) • Oh, What a Beautiful Mornin' (Gordon MacRae) • and more.
00119084 Vocal Transcriptions with Piano $19.99

MARIAH CAREY
Always Be My Baby • Dreamlover • Emotions • Heartbreaker • Hero • I Don't Wanna Cry • Love Takes Time • Loverboy • One Sweet Day • Vision of Love • We Belong Together • and more.
00306835 Vocal Transcriptions with Piano $19.95

PATSY CLINE
Always • Blue Moon of Kentucky • Crazy • Faded Love • I Fall to Pieces • Just a Closer Walk with Thee • Sweet Dreams • more. Also includes a biography.
00740072 Vocal Transcriptions with Piano $16.99

ELLA FITZGERALD
A-tisket, A-tasket • But Not for Me • Easy to Love • Embraceable You • The Lady Is a Tramp • Misty • Oh, Lady Be Good! • Satin Doll • Stompin' at the Savoy • Take the "A" Train • and more. Includes a biography and discography.
00740252 Vocal Transcriptions with Piano $16.95

JOSH GROBAN
Alejate • Awake • Believe • February Song • In Her Eyes • Now or Never • O Holy Night • Per Te • The Prayer • To Where You Are • Un Amore Per Sempre • Un Dia Llegara • You Are Loved (Don't Give Up) • You Raise Me Up • You're Still You • and more.
00306969 Vocal Transcriptions with Piano $19.99

GREAT FEMALE SINGERS
Cry Me a River (Ella Fitzgerald) • Crazy (Patsy Cline) • Fever (Peggy Lee) • How Deep Is the Ocean (How High Is the Sky) (Billie Holiday) • Little Girl Blue (Nina Simone) • Tenderly (Rosemary Clooney) • and more.
00307132 Vocal Transcriptions with Piano $19.99

GREAT MALE SINGERS
Can't Help Falling in Love (Elvis Presley) • Georgia on My Mind (Ray Charles) • I've Got the World on a String (Frank Sinatra) • Mona Lisa (Nat King Cole) • Ol' Man River (Paul Robeson) • What a Wonderful World (Louis Armstrong) • and more.
00307133 Vocal Transcriptions with Piano $19.99

BILLIE HOLIDAY
TRANSCRIBED FROM HISTORIC RECORDINGS
Billie's Blues (I Love My Man) • Body and Soul • Crazy He Calls Me • Easy Living • A Fine Romance • God Bless' the Child • Lover, Come Back to Me • Miss Brown to You • Strange Fruit • The Very Thought of You • and more.
00740140 Vocal Transcriptions with Piano $17.99

JAZZ DIVAS
A collection of 30 ballads recorded by Ella Fitzgerald, Billie Holiday, Diana Krall, Nina Simone, Sarah Vaughan, and more! Includes: Black Coffee • It Might as Well Be Spring • The Man I Love • My Funny Valentine • and more.
00114959 Vocal Transcriptions with Piano $19.99

LADIES OF CHRISTMAS
Grown-Up Christmas List (Amy Grant) • Hard Candy Christmas (Dolly Parton) • Merry Christmas, Darling (Karen Carpenter) • Rockin' Around the Christmas Tree (Brenda Lee) • Santa Baby (Eartha Kitt) • and more.
00312192 Vocal Transcriptions with Piano $19.99

NANCY LAMOTT
Autumn Leaves • Downtown • I Have Dreamed • It Might as Well Be Spring • Moon River • Skylark • That Old Black Magic • and more.
00306995 Vocal Transcriptions with Piano $19.99

LEONA LEWIS – SPIRIT
Better in Time • Bleeding Love • The First Time Ever I Saw Your Face • Here I Am • Homeless • I Will Be • I'm You • Whatever It Takes • Yesterday • and more.
00307007 Vocal Transcriptions with Piano $17.95

CHRIS MANN
Always on My Mind • Ave Maria • Cuore • Falling • Longer • My Way • Need You Now • On a Night like This • Roads • Unless You Mean It • Viva La Vida.
00118921 Vocal Transcriptions with Piano $16.99

MEN OF CHRISTMAS
The Christmas Song (Chestnuts Roasting on an Open Fire) (Nat King Cole) • A Holly Jolly Christmas (Burl Ives) • It's Beginning to Look like Christmas (Perry Como) • White Christmas (Bing Crosby) • and more.
00312241 Vocal Transcriptions with Piano $19.99

THE BETTE MIDLER SONGBOOK
Boogie Woogie Bugle Boy • Friends • From a Distance • The Glory of Love • The Rose • Some People's Lives • Stay with Me • Stuff like That There • Ukulele Lady • The Wind Beneath My Wings • and more, plus a fantastic bio and photos.
00307067 Vocal Transcriptions with Piano $19.99

THE BEST OF LIZA MINNELLI
And All That Jazz • Cabaret • Losing My Mind • Maybe This Time • Me and My Baby • Theme from "New York, New York" • Ring Them Bells • Sara Lee • Say Liza (Liza with a Z) • Shine It On • Sing Happy • The Singer • Taking a Chance on Love.
00306928 Vocal Transcriptions with Piano $19.99

ONCE
All the Way Down • Broken Hearted Hoover Fixer Sucker Guy • Fallen from the Sky • Falling Slowly • Gold • The Hill • If You Want Me • Leave • Lies • Once • Say It to Me Now • Trying to Pull Myself Away • When Your Mind's Made Up.
00102569 Vocal Transcriptions with Piano $16.99

FRANK SINATRA – MORE OF HIS BEST
Almost like Being in Love • Cheek to Cheek • Fly Me to the Moon • I Could Write a Book • It Might as Well Be Spring • Luck Be a Lady • Old Devil Moon • Somebody Loves Me • When the World Was Young • and more.
00307081 Vocal Transcriptions with Piano $19.99

THE VERY BEST OF FRANK SINATRA
Come Fly with Me • I've Got You Under My Skin • It Was a Very Good Year • My Way • Night and Day • Summer Wind • The Way You Look Tonight • You Make Me Feel So Young • and more. Includes biography.
00306753 Vocal Transcriptions with Piano $19.95

STEVE TYRELL – BACK TO BACHARACH
Alfie • Always Something There to Remind Me • Close to You • I Say a Little Prayer • The Look of Love • Raindrops Keep Fallin' on My Head • This Guy's in Love with You • Walk on By • and more.
00307024 Vocal Transcriptions with Piano $16.99

THE BEST OF STEVE TYRELL
Ain't Misbehavin' • I Concentrate on You • I've Got a Crush on You • Isn't It Romantic? • A Kiss to Build a Dream On • Stardust • You'd Be So Nice to Come Home To • and more.
00307027 Vocal Transcriptions with Piano $16.99

SARAH VAUGHAN
Black Coffee • If You Could See Me Now • It Might as Well Be Spring • My Funny Valentine • The Nearness of You • A Night in Tunisia • Perdido • September Song • Tenderly • and more.
00306558 Vocal Transcriptions with Piano $17.95

VOCAL POP
Bad Romance • Bleeding Love • Breathe • Don't Know Why • Halo • I Will Always Love You • If I Ain't Got You • Rehab • Rolling in the Deep • Teenage Dream • You Belong with Me • and more!
00312656 Vocal Transcriptions with Piano $19.99

ANDY WILLIAMS – CHRISTMAS COLLECTION
Blue Christmas • Do You Hear What I Hear • Happy Holiday • The Little Drummer Boy • O Holy Night • Sleigh Ride • What Are You Doing New Year's Eve? • and more. Includes a great bio!
00307158 Vocal Transcriptions with Piano $17.99

ANDY WILLIAMS
Can't Get Used to Losing You • The Days of Wine and Roses • The Hawaiian Wedding Song (Ke Kali Nei Au) • The Impossible Dream • Moon River • More • The Most Wonderful Time of the Year • Red Roses for a Blue Lady • Speak Softly, Love • A Time for Us • Where Do I Begin • and more.
00307160 Vocal Transcriptions with Piano $17.99

HAL•LEONARD® CORPORATION
7777 W. BLUEMOUND RD. P.O. BOX 13819 MILWAUKEE, WI 53213

www.halleonard.com
Prices, contents, and availability subject to change without notice.